Moments of Motherhood

Rohana Dewfall

BookLeaf Publishing

India | USA | UK

Presentation by *BookLeaf Publishing*

Web: www.bookleafpub.com

E-mail: info@bookleafpub.com

ISBN : 9789357446990

First edition 2021

DEDICATION

To my beautiful babies, Theodore, Ila-Rae and Ezra. I am grateful for everything.

ACKNOWLEDGEMENT

I want to thank my wonderful mum, Daya, for supporting me in every venture I take and reading over every draft nomatter the time of day.

Thank you to my incredible husband, for faith in me even when I have none, and for calling me crazy when I need to hear it.

Gemma, thank you for being the friend who's radically honest. Without your support, creating this wouldn't have been possible.

Thank you to my beautiful children, who every single day teach me more about the human I want to be, even if sometimes it's be showing me the kind of human I don't want to be. My greatest teachers, thank you.

PREFACE

Poems and photography go hand in hand as art, capturing the world in a light that may otherwise get lost. This collection of poems began as a journal, where I would document little snippets of life with my children. It is series of snapshots, where there's been a pause for reflection in the day, and a poem born from the moment.

Village

It takes a village to raise a child
That's what they said
But nobody mentioned
That for most here in the west
That village is all but dead.

I've learned in my years
As mama of one, two, three
That finding a village
Can sometimes be,
A tiresome task
When there's nobody to ask..
Where the village of children raisers has gone.

It's become a community online
A sign of the times
The village has moved
Onto squares and statuses

And we no longer are confined
By distance
Or time
We can connect with those who share our views
This online community
Brings hope and solidarity

But though the virtual space allows such
wonderful connection
The physical village is still gone and missed

And so behind the squares
And the picture perfect house
There may be a person crumbling
Under the load
A letter from a friend
A hug or a kiss
Something warming for the tummy
Is bliss.

The village as we knew it
Has long since gone
But here in its ashes there is hope
If we pause for a minute
And check in with ourselves
We might learn how to build a community again

Different this time
More suited to our world
Offering though, the much needed support

The village is dead
The village is gone
The village is missed
The village waits to be born

Play Mama

Play mama
Play diggers and dinosaurs
Play dress up and dance
Play with me
Play with us
Play so we can share with you
The wonder of our world
The joy we know you need

Play with us mama
Because we need to tell you
About all the feelings
We cannot express

Play with us mama
Please put the jobs down
We're only little right now
Take a breath

The dishes for later mama
Please come and play
We know you're tired
But please
Come play with us mama
Give us your time

It's all we ever really need

She's Busy Creating

She's busy creating,
What I don't know.
There will be paint and crayon
Following whereever she goes

Paper and stamps
Scissors and glue

She's creating constantly
And she's yet to be 2

I hope in my heart
Nomatter how frustrated I get,
With glue trails and paint marks
That I never forget

Her creativity matters
Far more than the mess
She's exploring the world
Theres no need to distress.

Puddles

Splash
I'm covered in mud
Mummy can you see me
Laughing loud

Splash
You do it too
Join in with me mummy
I promise it's fun

Splash
Splosh
Stomp

Splash
The mud will wash off
But my laughter will last
Forever ringing in your ears

Splash
I'm a little bit wet now
Mummy can you see
The mud splattered on my face
I'm thrilled

Splash
Splosh
Stomp

Splash
Thank you mummy
For joining in with me
We're both soaking and laughing
Together

Splash
It's one of my favourite memories
I hope we do it again and again
Playing in puddles
Forever

Cookies and Conversations

Conversations,
Held as we walk
And observe the world,
I'm amazed at my 4 year old.

Conversations
As we sit together,
With cookies and hot chocolate
I'm in awe as we talk

Conversations
On the bus ride home,
People spotting
Story plotting
I never knew I'd learn so much

Conversations
As we play with toys
With cookie crumbs scattered
The mess never matters
Because these are

The best conversations
I'll ever have

Clouds

The clouds are the mother of the earth
Did you know that mummy?

Because when the clouds rain
The earth grows.

Ally

He didn't like to talk to her much
She didn't understand,
She was filled with love for him
Her first great grandchild.

But his spirited personality
Meant he batted her away,
But when she left to go back home
He's asked when she'll come and stay.

Our children aren't performing monkeys
Or puppets we can master,
So though it was hard to see her sad
I chose his side before and after.

She's old and deserves respect
Says a voice inside my head.
He's young says my heart,
Still learning.
His needs matter more instead.

If can't be an ally to my child
There is no point in trying
To be an ally to other humans
When the one I grew isn't thriving.

So even though it might not be what "should" be
done
I'll let him have his say
Because loves still love regardless
Of whether the child says to come and play.

Feelings

It's okay darling
You're feeling hurt
Sad
It's okay darling
You're allowed to be mad

I won't try to fix it
Because honestly I can't
You need to feel the feelings
I will wait and chant,
Mantras that will get me through
This parenting rollercoaster
I'm right here by your side

"This too shall pass"
"One step at a time"
"It's hard for everyone right now"
"You can choose to laugh"

These mantras I tell myself
Again and again
I ground myself
Ready for when
The feelings are smaller

You want a hug
"Mummy I need you now"
I'll hold you snug

It's okay darling
You're feelin sad
It's okay darling
You're allowed to be mad.

Humans

My child is not a toy
Or a blank slate to be molded
My child is not bad
Or naughty to be scolded

His sister isn't mean
Her brother isn't rough

They're humans learning to live
And life can be tough

We criticise children
Without giving them their dues.
Children are among the most oppressed
Of our society - its not news.

We don't respect them
We constantly correct them
We tell them to stop, don't talk
We make them walk
Even when their tired

Our children's childhoods
Are endangered

And it's definitely our fault
Somehow we've forgotten
We're raising humans
And so we default,
To old age tactics of shame and blame.
To bribery and tears.
We seem to think our children won't be scarred,
By us belittling their fears.

My children are not blank slates
Or performing monkeys doing tricks
And neither are yours
Or yours.
Or yours.
They're humans
And raising them is politics.

Concerned

Concerned is a kind word
Often use in attempt
To help mothers who are deep in the river
Of the beautiful chaos that motherhood brings

But concern can seem patronising
When used without consideration
Because often times though the river may be
deep
We're learning to swim a different way

And concern may create a tide
That pulls us from our feet
While it continues to fuel
Systems of oppression

So consider please
Where you place your concern
Is it genuinely founded?
Or is perhaps your concern a way for you
To wash your hands of help more grounded,
In connection,
In support,
In love and caring thought.

Naked

Naked is a conversation that comes up a lot in
our house
Why can't we be Naked mummy
I'm not cold
I don't want clothes on

Naked is natural
Comfortable
Joyful and free

Naked brings confidence
Something I feel my generation lost
Something I think we were prevented from
having

For fear
Of "those people"
From fear of " you never know who is around"

It's no wonder we have lost touch with nature so
much
When being Naked offends.
When a Naked baby is considered risky
Playing outside with sticks and water

Our wildness is disappearing
The wild children are endangered
We've trapped them in uniforms
Made them conform
And labelled them when they don't.

Because when the wildness shows its face
When their Naked confidence blooms,
There is a threat
Disguised often by fear of "those people"
Who in fact are few and far between.
Exhaserbated by the media
To make sure we live in fear,
Because when we can't trust our neighbours,
Then we're alone throughout the years
That we need our village most.

Naked is a gift
And curse
It makes conversations heated

But please remember that my Naked children
Aren't a threat
They are wild
Confident
Content

Please don't rob their innocence
By trapping them in clothes.

My spirited children will not confrom
They prefer the ground beneath their toes.
Don't take away their joy
And relationship with body
Just because you don't understand
That they don't need to please anybody.

My Naked child is full of laughter
She's dancing with her soul.
My Naked child is filled with strength
He knows the power of his soul.
My Naked children are themselves
They have so much more to learn
But forcing them to cover up
Won't let their fires burn.

Dragons

You are dragons
Here to breathe fire
Hold us accountable
Rage at the world

You are dragons
Young and fierce
Setting little fires everywhere

My darling dragons
Breathe it all out
Rage
Roar
Rampage

Maybe when enough of you do
More people will listen

One, Two, Three

One
Two
Three

"You'll have your hands full"
He said as he walked past
"Why would you choose to have another"
She said in the park
"Goodness me you're busy"
Said the nurse
"Wow you're brave"
"I couldn't think of anything worse"

All the voices
Telling me why and why not
Lots of people weighing in
I think they forgot
How to use their manners
Or take Thumper's father's advice
"Don't say nothing at all,
If you can't say something nice."

Newborn Days

Motherhood
In the newborn days
Is soft and slow and sweet

But not many people talk about
About the haze the comes
(I'd feel it)
Almost defeat (me)
Some days anyway...

The mesh from day to week
The cycle on repeat

The newborn days are not the hardest
But they surely can be filled
With lonely isolation
For a new mother
Must rebuild
The version of herself
That she didn't know she'd lost
Or her mental health is the cost.
A new mother
Needs time
Needs friends
Needs love.

The newborn days
Are slow and soft and sweet
But don't be fooled by gorgeous pictures
They're hard too.
So when you meet
A newborn mother
Be tender
Be kind
Rememeber she's growing
She's learning to find
Her way
Slowly, softly, sweetly,
Among the milky breath
And little wrapped fingers in her hand
Among the newborn baby smell
The nappies
Cuddles
And
The hours that mesh from days to weeks
The newborn time moves swiftly
And then once again
Times will change
We blink and their voice comes
"Mama, lift me"

Octopus Hands

Mama your hands
I'm watching them move
They're always so busy
Connected to you.

You hold us and hug us
You squeeze our hands too
Your hands have magic
But you only have 2

Sometimes you say
That you don't have enough hands.
You'd like to be an octopus
And maybe then you'd feel that you can,
Cope with all the odd jobs
The comfort
The chaos
But mama more hands
Wouldn't be the same to us

Your limited hands
Mean you have to slow down
When we need a cuddle
Or help to calm down

Your hands hold the magic
After a scrape or a scratch
Mama your hands
Are the ones we know will catch
Us when we fall
Will help us reach up tall
Will glue the googly eyes onto rocks
And will stretch on our socks

So don't become an octopus mama
Please don't grow anymore hands
You're better as a human
Stay with us on the land.

Plaque Monsters

Time to brush teeth
The internal groan grows
The toddlers are fussing
And goodness knows...
We hate teeth brushing time
It's always a chore
But hold on a minute...
Not anymore.

"Ahhh, don't brush us away"
I put on a voice
"Stop kids, we want to stay"
There creeps a smile
As my defiant child thinks
I won't let those planque monsters
Make my mouth stink!

"Go away toothbrush"
My voice pretends to be scared
The story of plaque monsters
Is one well prepared

The smile turns to laughter
And a determined little boy

Picks up his toothbrush
And brushes with joy
As I shriek and I squeal
Pretending to be caught
"He's got us"
"Oh no"
They sound quite distraught

His teeth are now clean
Not bad for today
Thank goodness for stories
Helping hard situations feel okay.

I yelled

Today I yelled at you
My sweet sweet child,

I yelled.

You cried.

I saw your tears
And stopped.
I realised,
That though my big feeling were raging inside.
They were mine to feel not yours.

My darling boy I'm sorry
That
I projected my emotions
Without a pause.

Because when I pause
And breath
When I stop and look at you,
I see the hurt
My yelling caused

I was mad

And frustrated
And I began to let it out,
In a booming voice
With unkind words
My feelings came out in a shout.

I'm sorry darling
Really.
It wasn't about you.
These years are yours for learning
And I'm here to learn with you.

So I'll stop and hug you
Hold you tight
Apologise sincerely.

Because when I yelled
I caused you harm
I wasn't thinking clearly.

Though yes there are rules
We must try to keep,
It's my job to help
You do so.
We make mistakes.
We try again.
And we learn

Today I yelled

My sweet sweet child.
I yelled.
You cried.
We hugged.
We tried
Again.

Kind Please

Kind hands please
Kind feet please
Kind words please.

I ask to revert back to kindness
And then wonder why
Because when I feel frustrated
I want to shout and cry.

Let it out
Safely
Your feelings are valid
Please don't keep them inside

Kind hands and feet and words to people
Are great aims
For us to advise

But scream as loud as needed
Kick and hit pillows all you please
Stomp on the ground
Jump on the bed
Throw balls
Run
Dance

Scream
Cry

Say the unkind things
I can take it

You're only little after all.
I'm here for all your feeling
Be they big or be they small.

When I am mad
I can be mean
So why do I ask you
To revert back to kindness
When it's something I still struggle to do?

Breathe

Listening to my children breathe
In
Out
In
Out
In
Out

It's a reminder
I am enough

Ships in passing

My love
We've changed
Our family has grown
The time we had for each other
Each day has flown
(Away)

In between dinner and nappy changes
We briefly have a chat
I now understand why my mother,
Told me exactly that
This may happen.
Like it did for her.
"Ships in passing" she said...
These busy years are filled with fears
That time apart will shed
(Our connection).

But truly through the mess
Of daily life
I know,
There's nobody else we'd be on this road with
It's steady and it's slow.
It's chaos and it's beautiful
It's messy that is true

It's filled with love
For us
And them
I'm filled with love for you.

Love Letter

I visited my past today
And gave myself a hug
You can do this motherhood thing
I told myself
A reminder
Warm and snug

A future me came to now
And told me the same thing
A love letter of sorts I guess
A reminder to laugh and sing

If only we could be as kind
To our present self
As we
Are kind to our children
When we watch them wild and free

Future me held my hand
And told me of a time
Where I'd have space and miss the mess
Of song, and dance and rhyme.

I'm tired of criticising
I'm tired of all the 'to-dos'

Future me reminded me
That there's plenty of time for all those rules

Right now stop and listen
Hug the close
Hold them tight
They won't be in my bed forever
So I'll make the most of every night.